The
A–Z Guide
for Promoting
Your Self-Published Book

Brenda Strohbehn Henderson

ISBN: 1984169823
ISBN-13: 978-1984169822

To those who realize
that writing a book
requires equal amounts
of words
and hard work

CONTENTS

INTRODUCTION

Self-publishing your book can be an exciting and cost-effective way to make your book available to the general public. However, the book's promotion falls solely on you, the author. This little book contains twenty-six ideas for promoting your self-published book. Use the ones that apply to your audience, tweak those that need tweaking, and eliminate the ones that don't suit your needs.

Legally, I need to state that the use of this material does not guarantee the sale of your book. Personally, however, I have used several of these ideas for my own books, and I have found them to be effective and helpful. That's why I wanted to share them with you!

A – AUTHOR

Identify yourself as an author to initiate conversations that can lead to possible sales. That's who you are now—officially so! Avoid arrogance, but you should be confident in your role.

Notes and Ideas Regarding
My Role as an Author

B – BLOGGERS

Bloggers are influencers within their platform and readership. Offer a free copy of your book to a few influential bloggers in exchange for an honest review. (They must state that phrase in their review, or the review is legitimately considered by most as a "paid" review.) Additionally, offer to guest post or to do an interview on the blog—a mutually beneficial practice, because both of you bring your spheres of influence to one location.

Notes and Ideas Regarding Bloggers

C – COST

Cost matters. Charge what you would pay, not what you think it's worth! The royalties increase as the price goes up; however, the sales go down if the cost is too high, meaning that fewer royalties come in! Additionally, at the time of this writing, people generally prefer the ease of Amazon (and the free shipping available through Amazon Prime), so plan your promotions with that in mind.

Notes and Ideas Regarding Cost

D – DISCOUNTS

Discounts should be few and far between and should rarely be used within the first few months. Guard against giving large discounts right after initiating your sale of the book. People don't like being encouraged to buy the book right away and then finding out that those who waited got a better price! Avoid the "if you make it cheaper, they will come" mentality. Amazon often promotes your new release by offering a discount from the start. Let them. It doesn't affect your royalties, and they know how to do this!

Notes and Ideas Regarding Discounts

E – E-MAIL

Within the signature line of your e-mails, include the name of your book and a link to the purchase site. For example:

Joe and Brenda Henderson
Co-authors, *Petals of Promises* (on the title of the book, include the hyperlink to the book's Amazon page)

Notes and Ideas Regarding E-Mail Signature Lines

F – FACEBOOK, ETC.*

Facebook is an essential tool for marketing your book—*if* your readership frequents Facebook. Create an author page or a book-specific page so that the general public can have access to that information without having access to your personal life or photos. Keep current with your page, and people will follow you! Let it drop, and they'll drop you. Post short clips or quotations from your book, making sure to include the title of the book as the source of your quotation. This makes your post or status update "shareable" and helps you enlist the support of your readers in promoting your book.

*This same principle of promotion applies to Instagram, Twitter, and all current forms of social media.

Notes and Ideas Regarding the Use of Facebook

G – GENEROSITY

Generosity will be one of your greatest promotional tools, but it must be sincere. If you want people to "share" your Facebook posts, share a few of theirs. If you want people to comment on your status, blog post, or article, generously comment on theirs (but again, only in a sincere way). People will bend over backward for you until or unless they realize that you are all about *you*. Then it's all bets off! Truly care and be excited about learning from others. The added assistance they will give you in return is merely a bonus!

Notes and Ideas Regarding Generosity

H – HELP

There is something in your book that will help someone else. Emphasize that. Share that. Focus on that. This also lets readers know that you are more concerned about what's in it for *them* than you are about what's in it for *you*. And that matters to them.

Notes and Ideas Regarding Helping Others

I – IMAGINATION

As generic as it sounds, use your imagination to come up with book-specific ideas. Ask yourself: "What would make *me* buy this book?" Then let your imagination run wild, temper the ideas to fit your time, your budget, and your locale, and know no limits on the possibilities.

Notes and Ideas Regarding Imagination

J – JOURNEY

Publishing your book, as you know by now, is a journey, not a destination. Constantly seek new ways to promote your book and utilize your contacts, connections, skills, abilities, etc. to do so. There's not a one-time magic formula for success other than to maintain a forward momentum.

Notes and Ideas Regarding the Journey

K – KINFOLK

Your family members will be your personal PR team! Be careful not to use your relationship to them to push your way into their world, but ask them if they would be willing to help by opening the doors for you and introducing you to those within their circles.

Notes and Ideas Regarding Enlisting the Help of My Family (Kinfolk)

L – LIBRARIES

Libraries love to encourage authors and readers! Start by contributing a copy of your book to your local library. While you're there, see if they may be interested in having a book signing event or a book reading (if it's short).

Notes and Ideas Regarding Libraries

M – MAIL

Handwritten notes are nearly a lost art form, which is what makes them special. Take an evening to write post cards or short notes to those who have helped you or who have a need that your book can meet. People can't buy your book until they know that it exists.

Notes and Ideas Regarding the Use of Mail

N – NEWSPAPERS

Contact someone in the office of your local newspaper to let them know about your book's release. Offer to do an interview with one of their reporters or to write an article on the subject matter of your book.

Notes and Ideas Regarding Newspapers

O – OFFERS

Offer a "bonus" to readers for assisting with your promotion. For example, have readers on Facebook "share" the link to your book to be registered for a giveaway for something like a Starbucks card or an Amazon card. Sending a $5.00 gift card via e-mail is well worth the revenue that may be generated with their help.

Notes and Ideas Regarding Offers

P – PEOPLE

People are your best promotional tool. However, they should not be *used*; they should be *utilized*!

Notes and Ideas Regarding People

Q – QUICK NOTES

Use notes, social media updates, e-mails, etc. that are quick to write and quick to read. Keep your name and the name of your book (and where that book can be found) in front of people. They don't want your family history, nor do they need to know all the struggles you overcame to write the book. They need to know, in one brief sentence, what's in it for them. Practice keeping it simple!

Notes and Ideas Regarding Quick Notes

R – REVIEWS

Reviews help! Graciously ask purchasers for an honest review of your book—particularly on Amazon (they need to have purchased the book through Amazon to make it a legitimate review).

Notes and Ideas Regarding Reviews

S – SOUND BITES

Think, write, and speak in terms of sound bites. Think this way: If they were to interview me for television, what would I want the "teaser" sound bite to be? Those are the teasers that you should post on social media sites, include in the signature line of your e-mails, and use as branding tools for your book, series, or author site.

Notes and Ideas Regarding Sound Bites

T – TEACHERS

Teachers are great promoters of books! Give a copy of your book to a few of your favorite and most influential teachers. Be sure to include a note of thanks. Their promotion of your book is not your motivation; it is a blessing they can choose to bestow or to withhold.

Notes and Ideas Regarding Teachers

U – UNIFORMITY

Uniform font, color, and style are important branding tools for your promotion. Ideally, people will begin to think of you or of your book when they see your logo, cover photo, font, etc.

Notes and Ideas Regarding Uniformity

V – VISTAPRINT*

I'm a sucker for Vistaprint, because they make it ridiculously easy to buy things related to my blog or to the books I want to promote. Vistaprint.com is a great source for book-related post cards, author business cards, apparel, or fun "extras" to use as giveaways (e.g., I once gave their "stress balls" to all of my author friends for Christmas). Only buy what you'll use, though, because some of it is just "stuff" that will get lost in the shuffle. The goal is to stand out in the sea of authors vying for the attention of your readers.

*I am not on commission with Vistaprint, nor am I an affiliate for them. They're just a company whose product I appreciate!

Notes and Ideas Regarding Vistaprint

W – WEBSITE

If you don't have a website for your book or as an author site, be sure to have an author page or book-specific account on Facebook, Instagram, Twitter, or other form of social media. People need to know where to find you. MichaelHyatt.com provides the easiest and most practical short video on how to set up a website in about twenty minutes. I used it as my guide, and at one time I owned five websites. They are worth every penny. But you can also set one up for free, and there's nothing wrong with those either!

Watch the video: MichaelHyatt.com/ez-wordpress-setup/

X – *X* MARKS THE SPOT

This should be true of each reference to your book. "Mark the spot" with a hyperlink, a notation, or a written URL where people can find a copy to purchase. The more they have to do to find it, the less likely they are to purchase. Make it easy for them to purchase by marking the spot clearly!

Notes and Ideas Regarding Marking the Spot

Y – YULETIDE

Promote your book as a yuletide gift (or as a birthday gift, graduation gift, etc.). Remind readers that Amazon will gift wrap (minimal fee) and/or include a gift note (free)!

Notes and Ideas Regarding Yuletide Promotions

Z – ZEAL

Your zeal (ardent passion) will inspire others, and they will want more of that passion and inspiration. If you are timid about your book, it communicates that your book is not worth reading. Passion for your topic and for the need it meets, the solution it provides, or the enjoyment it brings is contagious! Use this final promotional tool often!

Notes and Ideas Regarding Zeal

CONCLUSION

The world of social media and the realm of publishing possibilities change almost daily. These ideas may be obsolete before I hit the "submit" button! Therefore, I urge you to "strike while the iron is hot."

I wish you the very best in your writing and publishing endeavors.

Keep writing!

ABOUT THE AUTHOR

Brenda Strohbehn Henderson launched her faith-based blog, *Petals from the Basket*, in March 2012. As a woman who married for the first time at the age of fifty-five, Brenda brings a unique insight to the needs, joys, and concerns of women of all ages and from every marital status.

Brenda and her husband, Joe (with whom she co-authored *Petals of Promises: A 365-Day Devotional for Women*), reside in Indiana, where they are active in their local church and enjoy writing, fishing in neighboring ponds, spending time with family, entertaining, and cheering on the Notre Dame football team!

ALSO BY BRENDA STROHBEHN HENDERSON
(Available via Amazon and Barnes and Noble)

Petals from the Basket

Petals from the Basket (Book 2)

Petals from the Basket (Book 3)

Petals of Gratitude

Choosing to Change when Change Happens

Petals of Promises